The 9 Secrets of Spiritually Successful People

by Sarah Bowling

Marilyn Hickey Ministries
P.O. Box 17340
Denver, CO 80217

The 9 Secrets
of Spiritually
Successful People

ISBN 1-56441-037-4

Unless otherwise noted,
all verses are taken from the
New International Version of the Bible.

Printed in the United States of America

Unit Four - (Matthew 5:14-16)

To all perfection I see a limit; but your commands are boundless. Oh, how I love your law! I meditate on it all day long (Psalms 119:96,97).

Secrets

Introduction

Though it was given nearly 2,000 years ago, the Sermon on the Mount has some very rich material in it for us today. The introduction to the Sermon, called the Beatitudes, is abundant in both its revelation and its application to our daily lives. However, for years, whenever I read them, I viewed the beatitudes as simply an unclear preface to the real meat of the Sermon on the Mount. Consequently, I just skimmed over them, and generally disregarded them.

Sometimes I tried to find meaning from the beatitudes to apply to my life, but they honestly just seemed to be a jumble of confusing words. Nevertheless, I knew there were some very rich and

There are two areas of **danger** of which you need to be aware!

1. The first danger is that this workbook may be so enticing that you may move too quickly through it, not really letting the power of the beatitudes transform you.

2. The second area of danger is that you may become so totally addicted to the beatitudes that you won't be able to *stop* meditating on the Sermon on the Mount. It's thoroughly RICH!

YOU HAVE BEEN WARNED!

practical spiritual truths in the beatitudes. My frustration continued until I began to meditate on them. Then, the beatitudes came alive as the Holy Spirit taught me how to apply them to my life.

Are you lacking spiritual fervor in your life? Do you understand the balance between God's holiness and His mercy? Has your spiritual life become cold or diluted? If you answered "yes" to any of these questions, or if you are simply wanting greater intimacy with God...**this is the book for you!**

God has answers that will help you on a daily basis with the issues with which you struggle. No problem is bigger than God, and many of His solutions for your life can be found in the beatitudes.

Come with me into a greater depth in God. Let's wade into God's deep, but simple truths that never fail to revolutionize our lives!

> *As the man went eastward with a measuring line in his hand, he measured off a thousand cubits and then led me through water that was ankle-deep. He measured off another thousand cubits and led me through water that was knee-deep. He measured off another thousand and led me through water that was up to the waist. He measured off another thousand, but now it was a river that I could not cross, because the water had risen and was deep enough to swim in—a river that no one could cross . . . Swarms of living creatures will live wherever the river flows (Ezekiel 47:3-5, 9a).*

Let's Go!

Notes

_____

_____

_____

_____

_____

_____

_____

_____

_____

_____

_____

_____

_____

_____

_____

_____

_____

_____

_____

_____

_____

_____

_____

Notes

_____

_____

_____

_____

_____

_____

_____

_____

_____

_____

_____

_____

_____

_____

_____

_____

_____

_____

_____

_____

_____

_____

_____

_____

_____

Notes

Secrets

Unit One

Your goal for
this week is to
memorize
Matthew 5:1-3.

"Now when he saw the crowds, he went up on a mountainside and sat down. His disciples came to him, and he began to teach them, saying: 'Blessed are the poor in spirit, for theirs is the kingdom of heaven'" (Matthew 5:1-3).

Oh, how I love your law! I meditate on it all day long (Psalms 119:97).

Secrets

Lesson 1

Meditation is a major key to spiritual growth. If you desire to develop into the strong man or woman of God that He has called you to be, it is crucial that you learn how to meditate in the Word of God.

Let's talk about meditating so that we are on common ground. It will be helpful, first, to understand what godly meditating **is not**.

Meditating on God's Word *is not*:
- an "escape" from one's circumstances
- mindless repetition of short phrases
- emptying one's self of everything possible
- simply memorizing Scripture passages
- chanting

- assuming an unusual position for spiritual illumination
- detaching your mind from reality for short amounts of time

Meditating on God's Word *is*:
- bringing God into one's circumstances
- applying treasures from God's Word to daily life
- filling one's self with God's living, active, and effective Word
- more than just memorizing; it is taking God's Word into one's heart
- easy to do regardless of your location or physical position
- a powerful way to gain a deeper understanding of reality from God's perspective
- the avenue through which prosperity and success come,

   Do not let this Book of the Law depart from your mouth; meditate on it day and night, so that you may be careful to do everything written in it. Then you will be prosperous and successful (Joshua 1:8).

Let's look at what David, a man after God's own heart (Acts 13:22), had to say about the value of meditating:

Blessed is the man who does not walk in the counsel of the wicked or stand in the way of sinners or sit in the seat of mockers. But his delight is in the law of the LORD, and on his law he meditates day and night. He is like a tree planted by streams of water, which yields its fruit in season and whose leaf does not wither. Whatever he does prospers (Psalms 1:1-3).

Notice in the first verse that David talks about us walking, standing, and sitting. The important issue is in choosing *where* we walk, sit, and stand. We may choose to walk, sit, and/or stand with mockers, willful sinners, or in the counsel of the ungodly. However, we must also realize that these "locations" are not connected with a state of blessing.

Moving on to verse two, we see a person who

sits, stands, and walks in the Word—a person who **meditates on the Word**. Then, in verse 3, we are told the rewards of meditating on the Word.

The person who meditates on the Word:
- has great stability—*like a tree planted by streams of water*
- has constant access to fresh supplies—*by streams of water*
- is a productive and fruitful person—*yields its fruit in season*
- understands godly timing—*in season*
- has life continually coursing throughout every area of his life—*whose leaf does not wither*
- prospers in whatever he does

To make it simple, a person who meditates on the Word has stability and fresh supply in God, is productive and fruitful, understands godly timing, virtually overflows with life, and is prosperous in whatever he does.

Hit the mark for godly success— **MEDITATE ON GOD'S WORD!!!**

Q&A

1. On the following list, please mark out the things that you **do not want** to have in your life:

laziness	fresh supply of God
indecision	poverty
godly timing	instability
stability	doom
great achievements	wastefulness
deception	fullness of life
continual defeat	prosperity
intimacy with God	haphazard achievements

2. List the things that you did not cross out:

_____

_____

_____

_____

_____

_____

_____

3. Now, reread Psalms 1:1-3:

Blessed is the man who does not walk in the counsel of the wicked or stand in the way of sinners or sit in the seat of mockers. But his delight is in the law of the LORD,

and on his law he meditates day and night. He is like a tree planted by streams of water, which yields its fruit in season and whose leaf does not wither. Whatever he does prospers.

4. According to these verses, how can you acquire the things on the list you wrote out?

_____

_____

_____

_____

_____

_____

_____

_____

_____

_____

_____

Notes

_____
_____
_____
_____
_____
_____
_____
_____
_____
_____
_____
_____
_____
_____
_____
_____
_____
_____
_____
_____
_____
_____
_____
_____
_____

Notes

_____

_____

_____

_____

_____

_____

_____

_____

_____

_____

_____

_____

_____

_____

_____

_____

_____

_____

_____

_____

_____

_____

_____

_____

_____

Notes

Notes

Commit to the LORD whatever you do, and your plans will succeed (Proverbs 16:3).

Secrets

Lesson 2

In order to receive the *greatest* benefit from your time, effort, and money, I want to discuss the importance of completing this study. Whether you have just begun a wonderful relationship with Christ or have been in His family for a long time, it is important to get to know Him. One of the best ways to grow increasingly acquainted with Him is through His Word. There is no better way to get to know someone than to listen to their words and let those words sink into your heart.

Do you remember the first time you ever "fell in love"? Do you remember how you savored the other person's words, and let those words settle into your thinking? In a similar way, Jesus is waiting on you to give Him the opportunity to let His Word become the delight of your heart. In order to get the full benefit of His Word, we need to commit ourselves to letting it settle into us. It's hard for a love relationship with God to develop into anything of  substance if we don't commit to listening, interacting, and esteeming His Word. Therefore, I want to challenge you to use this workbook as a means of growing in Christ. This workbook, along with your commitment to complete all of the questions and exercises, will help you progress into a deeply intimate and closer walk with God!

Let me also challenge you to provide God with the opportunity to reveal Himself to you by completing this workbook. If you approach Him in a nonchalant and casual way, do not expect to have a very deep relationship with Him. As in any relationship with depth, both parties must commit to that relationship. God has committed Himself to being close to you, and He awaits the walking out of your commitment to Him.

If you will commit to meditate on the verses and make your way through this workbook, you will come to know Christ in a more intimate way than you now know Him. I know this because it says in Isaiah 55:10-11,

> *As the rain and the snow come down from heaven, and do not return to it without watering the earth and making it bud and flourish, so that it yields seed for the sower and bread for the eater,*
> **so is my word that goes out from my mouth: It will not return to me empty, but will accomplish what I desire and achieve the purpose for which I sent it.**

The commitment that will reap the most fruit from this study is as follows:

#1 Commit to go through and finish each lesson— 10-20 minutes daily/5 days a week.

#2 Commit to meditate (memorize, personalize, and visualize) the 16 verses pertaining to this study over the next 6-8 weeks.

#3 Commit to let God change you and mold you into His image, while He reveals Himself to you in greater depth.

The first item listed above is fairly self-explanatory. Meditating is something you will need to do as you can, utilizing free minutes throughout your day whenever possible.

Additionally, I will give you helpful ideas throughout this workbook that will help you successfully accomplish point number two. Realize from the outset that if you have a fairly demanding schedule, there may be times when you won't get your verse done for the day.

Don't give up! There will be other days when you will be able to do a little more than a single verse. We will not be moving at a "breakneck" speed. It is our goal to meditate on 16 verses for the next 6-8 weeks. This is not an overwhelming nor unreasonable goal—particularly when we are seeking to let God change us and to develop greater intimacy with Him. The third point is also self-explanatory.

Don't be intimidated by these goals. My

objective in this lesson is to encourage you to commit to finish what you start so that you will obtain a more absorbing walk with God. Please read the statement below, and if you feel comfortable doing so, sign and date it as an indication of your agreement to complete this workbook and its assignments to the best of your ability without allowing yourself any of the "usual" variety of excuses.

---

*To the best of my ability, I agree to meditate on Matthew 5:1-16 and complete this workbook with all of its assignments. I will allow God to change me and develop greater intimacy with Him **through His grace,** to the best of my ability.*

_____
Signature

_____
Date

Notes

_____
_____
_____
_____
_____
_____
_____
_____
_____
_____
_____
_____
_____
_____
_____
_____
_____
_____
_____
_____
_____
_____

Notes

Notes

Today's verse is *"Now when he saw the crowds, he went up on a mountainside and sat down. His disciples came to him,..."* (Matthew 5:1)

Secrets

Lesson 3

Now, let's look at the meaning of **meditate**. Meditation has three parts. If you ever played sports, you may have received an award called the M.V.P.—the Most Valuable Player. When it comes to the

"game of life," there's no more valuable player on your team than the Word of God. The more you meditate on the Word, the greater impact it has on you. Meditating on the Word is truly your "Most Valuable Player" —your M.V.P.

The M.V.P. of meditating has three parts:

Memorize • Visualize • Personalize

The first step in meditating on the Word is to memorize. Now, let's make it very practical with today's verse, Matthew 5:1. I find the easiest way to meditate is to begin my new verse at night, right before I go to bed. Then, in bed, I review my newly learned verse (even though it's usually not 100% perfect) a few times before I go to sleep. As I sleep, my brain is going over the new verse so that when I look at it in the morning, it "sticks to my ribs" much more readily.

Whenever you see an alarm clock, **STOP** and read the helpful suggestions. You'll get some good ideas for effective meditation.

Throughout my day, I work on my new verse and, generally, by the evening I know my verse for the day fairly well.

Sometimes, I'll have a verse that's longer than usual, or

I'll have a difficult time getting it. I don't let that frustrate me. I just keep chipping away at it, regardless of how slowly I progress. Ultimately I will get the verse memorized. The key is that I don't let myself get discouraged with my pace. I just keep plodding along, continuing to let the Word chip away at me.

In the next lesson, we will begin to study and put to use the various meanings of **meditate**. Right now, I want to encourage you to begin working on your verse regardless of where you are in your day. Be sure to focus particularly on it right before you go to bed. Today's verse is Matthew 5:1.

> **My eyes stay open through the watches of the night, that I may meditate on your promises (Psalms 119:148).**

For your convenience, we have put all the verses on pages at the back of this workbook. Take time now to cut them out, or zerox them to have ready to carry with you during the day.

Q&A

1. Take a moment at this point to pray, asking Jesus to help you be a teachable student for the time you will spend in this workbook. Ask Him to help you hear His voice clearly and distinctly while you are meditating upon His Word.

2. Write your prayer below.

_____

_____

_____

_____

_____

_____

_____

_____

_____

_____

_____

Notes

Notes

Notes

Notes

Today's verse is
Matthew 5:2:
*"...and he began
to teach them,
saying:..."*

Secrets

Lesson 4

As we talk about meditating on the Word, we need to realize that meditating is much more than simply memorizing, and consequently has more benefits than just learning for memory's sake. The goal of meditating on the Word is to let God's Word settle and take root in the deepest core of who we are, allowing it to conform us to Jesus' likeness!

In the last lesson, we talked about the **M.V.P.** of meditating, with the "**M**" being to memorize. However, merely memorizing is like deciding to eat an orange and peeling it without tasting its delicious fruit. In my opinion, simply memorizing God's Word without attempting to squeeze further life and application out of it is a tragedy. God's Word is meant to dig into us, take root and produce fruit through us. Simply memorizing the Word is like scattering seeds on concrete—they will not bear much fruit.

The next part of meditating in our **M.V.P.** lineup is the "**V,**" which stands for visualizing. When you visualize your verse, you put yourself into the verse and you see it happen—you put your verse into 3-D.

Let's look at the two verses we are learning thus far, and put **visualization** to work.

Matthew 5:1-2, *"Now when he saw the crowds, he went up on a mountainside and sat down. His disciples came to him, and he began to teach them, saying:..."*

1. Do your best to say these verses aloud without looking. Look only when you need a little help.

2. Now, put yourself in the crowd with Jesus. See

yourself being jostled while trying to get as close to Him as you possibly can.

3. Notice that some of the people leave when Jesus begins to teach, as if they were expecting some form of entertainment. Are you one of those who leaves, or are you one of those who stays?

4. Ask yourself, "Am I one of Jesus' disciples?" If your answer is yes, then picture yourself following Jesus up the mountainside. If your answer is no, please take a moment to consider God's goodness in your life. I would encourage you to pray the following, meaning it with everything in you:

Dear Jesus,

I believe that You died for me and that You rose again on the third day. I confess to You that I am a sinner and that I need Your love and forgiveness. Come into my life, forgive my sins, and give me eternal life. I confess You now as my Lord. Thank You for my salvation!

Signed_____ Date_____

(If you write to us and tell us of your decision to accept Jesus as your Lord and Savior, we will send you information to help you with your new life in Christ. See address at the end of workbook.)

5. Now see yourself sitting as close to Jesus as you can and listening to Him teach. Your attention is entirely captivated by Jesus.

List some of your thoughts on the way Jesus handled Himself in this situation.

_____

_____

_____

_____

_____

_____

_____

_____

_____

_____

_____

_____

_____

_____

_____

_____

_____

_____

_____

A TESTIMONY

One time, we had several people coming to visit from out of town, and I was to escort them on a one-day tour through our church and ministry building. These friends were very gracious people, but needed a lot of assistance from me in making the practical arrangements for their trip. Consequently, they kept calling and asking me to do "extra" things for them. Soon, I noticed that I was developing a bad attitude about helping these nice people. I knew this was displeasing to God, and I wanted to have the right attitude but, as much as I tried, I just was not able to **make** myself have a godly attitude. I was frustrated.

At the time, I was meditating on some verses in I Peter 4. The verse I was working on (or rather, the verse that was working on me) was I Peter 4:9, *"Offer hospitality to one another without grumbling."* As I began to meditate on this verse and let it soak into me, I noticed that I no longer had to work to maintain the right attitude. It was as if someone had turned a switch on in me. Suddenly, it was the most natural thing for me *to want* to help my friends. Thank God for His life-changing Word!

Q&A

1. Read through the testimony on the previous page. Have you experienced a similar life-changing effect from God's Word?

_____

_____

_____

_____

_____

_____

_____

_____

2. List some other areas where you recognize the need for the Word to change you.

_____

_____

_____

_____

_____
_____
_____
_____

Ask God to give you fruit from this study that accurately reflects His life-changing power in your life.

3. Write down the memory verses for yesterday and today on the lines below:

_____
_____
_____
_____
_____
_____
_____

Enlist a "Meditation Partner" who will join you in learning these verses.

Notes

_____

_____

_____

_____

_____

_____

_____

_____

_____

_____

_____

_____

_____

_____

_____

_____

_____

_____

_____

_____

_____

_____

_____

_____

Notes

_____
_____
_____
_____
_____
_____
_____
_____
_____
_____
_____
_____
_____
_____
_____
_____
_____
_____
_____
_____
_____
_____
_____
_____
_____

Notes

Today's verse is Matthew 5:3: *"Blessed are the poor in spirit, for theirs is the kingdom of heaven."*

Secrets

Lesson 5

Let's look at our verse for today, and provide the Holy Spirit an opportunity to apply this verse to our lives. First, we'll examine the meaning for *"blessed"* since that is a key word that shows up in almost each verse on which you will be meditating.

Blessed in the Greek *(makarios)* simply means "happy or blessed." In the Greek, the word *makarios* is a compound word comprised of the word *ma* meaning "not" and the word *keer* meaning "fate or death." Together, these two words could simply mean "no death—immortality, ever-alive, or lacking death." (Taken from *Adam Clarke Commentary.*)

As you are learning your verses over the next several weeks, it might be fun to make a collage—pictures cut from magazines and pasted on posterboard that remind you in some way of the verses you are depositing in your heart.

Let's apply this meaning to Psalms 112:1, *"Praise the LORD. Blessed is the man...who finds great delight in his commands."* The man who delights in the Word is blessed or lacks death. Therefore, as we implement the Word into our lives, the effect of the principle of death has a steadily decreasing effect upon us. Truly, as we walk in and apply the Word, we are both blessed and happy!

We understand that the word *blessed* is a state of blessing that dispels the principle of death as we walk in the Word. Next, we'll look at the phrase *poor in spirit.* What does it mean to be *poor in spirit?*

Circle the correct meanings of *poor* in the following list and cross out the incorrect meanings:

wealthy	destitute	abundance
average	middle-class	meager
needy	rich	deficient

To be poor means "to lack, to be in need." To be *poor in spirit* means "to lack in one's spirit." In other words, to be poor in spirit is to realize a deficiency in one's heart.

In order to realize we are poor, we must first recognize wealth. The people who are poor in spirit are those who recognize that something within is lacking. They realize their state of need.

We were created to crave our Creator.

God created man to need Him. He created us *poor in spirit*—with a "deficiency in our hearts." Unfortunately, we can stifle that heart-cry to connect with and draw from Him, convincing ourselves that we don't lack anything. Jesus said it is important for us to recognize and acknowledge our neediness so that we can inherit the kingdom of heaven.

Q&A

1. Based upon verse 3, fill in the blanks, using your name, you, your…and then reread what you have completed.

"Blessed are the poor in spirit, for theirs is the kingdom of heaven."

_____ (your name), you are blessed

when _____ recognize _____

spiritual need, for _____ is the kingdom

of heaven.

2. Do you have the first three verses committed to memory? Recite them to someone sometime today.

A PERSONAL EXAMPLE

In my travels when I was growing up, I saw many people living in poverty, and my heart really went out to them.  However, I also noticed that they did not seem to be troubled by their poverty and appeared to be rather happy. I asked my dad about this and he explained that because the people had never experienced the "wealth" enjoyed in richer countries, they didn't realize that they were "poor."

Remember:
Add your new verse to the previous verses when you are memorizing.

Notes

Notes

Notes

_____
_____
_____
_____
_____
_____
_____
_____
_____
_____
_____
_____
_____
_____
_____
_____
_____
_____
_____
_____
_____
_____

9 Secrets

Unit Two

Your goal for this week is to memorize Matthew 5:4-8.

"Blessed are those who mourn, for they will be comforted. Blessed are the meek, for they will inherit the earth. Blessed are those who hunger and thirst for righteousness, for they will be filled. Blessed are the merciful, for they will be shown mercy. Blessed are the pure in heart, for they will see God" (Matthew 5:4-8).

Today's verse is
Matthew 5:4:
*"Blessed are those
who mourn, for they
will be comforted."*

Secrets

Lesson 6

Today, we are concluding our discussion and application of the word *meditate*. Over the last few lessons, we talked about the **M.V.P.** of meditating and how the *"M"* represents memorize and the *"V"* stands for visualizing.

The *"P"* represents the word *"personalize."* When we talk about personalizing, we mean applying the verse and passage to oneself by actually using words that make the verse *personal*. Let me use an example. A friend once told me something very powerful. He said, **"God can do through you what you cannot do."** When I first heard the statement, it sounded nice. However, as I began to think about it and to personalize it, it became increasingly powerful. I examined the

PRACTICE "P"

**"God can do through you what
you cannot do."**

1. I put myself into the statement: "God can do through **Sarah** what **she** cannot do."
2. I thought about that for awhile, applying it to some seemingly impossible situations. Then I took another step, personalizing the statement a little more: "God can do through **me** what **I** cannot do."
3. Finally, I took this personalizing exercise a step further by looking upward to God and saying/thinking the statement: "**You** can do through **me** what **I** cannot do."

Now, the statement is very real and invigorating to me!

statement a few different ways to make it more personal.

Let's do a step-by-step walk-through of your verses with personalizing in mind.

Matthew 5:1-3, *"Now when he saw the crowds, he went up on a mountainside and sat down.* **His disciples** *came to him, and he began to teach* **them**, *saying: 'Blessed are the poor in spirit, for theirs is the kingdom of heaven.' "*

- First, notice the **bold-faced** words.

- In the following verses, fill in your name and the appropriate pronoun like I did in step one above. Be sure to read the "revised" passage after you have filled in the blanks:

  Matthew 5:1-4, *"Now when he saw the crowds, he went up on a mountainside and sat down.* _____ *(your name) came to him, and he began to teach* _____, *(pronoun) saying: 'Blessed are the poor in spirit, for theirs is the kingdom of heaven. Blessed are those who mourn, for they will be comforted.'"*

- Then, just as we did in step two, fill in the blanks with the more "personalizing" appropriate words, such as I, me, my. Be sure to read the verses after you have filled in the blanks.

BIBLE NOTE

Jesus began His ministry in a time when Judaism had become hardened by religious tradition and ritual. The religious leaders were very concerned with outward show, neglecting the hearts and motives of men entirely. Jesus spoke directly to the issues of motive, heart and soul condition, and fellowship with God.

The Sermon on the Mount was one of the earliest large public discourses Jesus gave. Most likely, the crowds came because they heard of the miracles Jesus was performing. Imagine their amazement when Jesus spoke to them about pureness of heart, righteousness, and meekness. These were not exactly the popular topics of the day!

Matthew 5:1-4, *"Now when he saw the crowds, he went up on a mountainside and sat down. _____ came to him, and he began to teach_____, saying: 'Blessed are the poor in spirit, for theirs is the kingdom of heaven. Blessed are those who mourn, for they will be comforted.' "*

- Finally, just like we did in step three, fill in the blanks with the more "personalizing" appropriate words, particularly in relation to Jesus such as you, I, me, my, etc.

Matthew 5:1-4, *"Now when _____ **(you)** saw the crowds, _____ went up on a mountainside and sat down. _____ **(I)** came to _____, and _____ began to teach _____ , saying: 'Blessed are the poor in spirit, for theirs is the kingdom of heaven. Blessed are those who mourn, for they will be comforted.'"*

Be sure to read the statement you just filled in and take a minute to let its full meaning sink into your soul.

Frankly, I don't know anyone who considers "mourning" a blessing. However, when we look at what happens with mourning in relation to the preceding verse that you've been working on, and it's outcome, it is truly a **blessing!**

When Jesus spoke of mourning, He was building on the thought that He began in the previous statement. Write the first beatitude in the following space.

_____

_____

_____

_____

_____

_____

_____

_____

_____

If you study the Greek word translated *mourn* in Matthew 5:4, you'll see that it is generally used in the New Testament in the context of being sorrowful due to a recognized lack. In other words, someone is sad because he is missing something and he realizes that he personally lacks the ability to fill the need.

Jesus here is speaking of those who recognize their lack and are sad because of their inability to fill their lack. These are the people who will be comforted.

The word *comforted* comes from the Greek word *paraklete* which is the same word used by Jesus when He was referring to the Holy Spirit. You open the door for God to do something—such as sending the Holy Spirit into your life to help you—when you first recognize your natural poverty of spirit and your basic human inability to fill your deficiency. At this point, the Holy Spirit comes in and you are **TRULY BLESSED!**

Caution: don't go so fast that you miss what God is saying to you!!! Savor the flavor!

Q&A

1. List some times or areas in your life where you have tried to be entirely self-sufficient with **no** input from God.

_____

_____

_____

_____

_____

_____

_____

_____

_____

_____

_____

_____

_____

_____

_____

_____

2. How successful were you in those endeavors?

_____

_____

_____

_____

_____

_____

3. List some times when you have allowed the Holy Spirit to come alongside and minister to you to fill the "hole in your heart."

_____

_____

_____

_____

_____

_____

_____

_____

Tell today's memory verse to someone.

Notes

_____

_____

_____

_____

_____

_____

_____

_____

_____

_____

_____

_____

_____

_____

_____

_____

_____

_____

_____

_____

_____

_____

Notes

Notes

Today's verse is
Matthew 5:5:
*"Blessed are the
meek, for they will
inherit the earth."*

Secrets

Lesson 7

In the last lesson, we discussed personalizing your verses. As a quick review, please write next to the letters what they represent in relation to meditating:

M _____

V _____

P_____

Keep a set of memory verses in your overcoat pocket during the winter or your sunglass case in the summer. That way, they will be with you during those spare moments of the day you usually spend in mindless waiting.

REVIEW

Now we are going to look at how this lesson's verse can be applied in our lives. First, to review, please answer the following questions based upon the previous lessons:

1. What does it mean to be poor in spirit?

_____

_____

_____

_____

_____

_____

_____

_____

_____

2. Can a person who considers himself self-sufficient, in God's reality, *really* be poor in spirit?

_____

_____

_____

_____

_____

_____

_____

_____

_____

3. Who were you designed to crave?

_____

_____

_____

_____

_____

_____

_____

_____

_____

Let's look at our verse for this lesson. Cross out the words that you do **NOT** associate with "meek."

Greedy	Arrogant	Self-centered
Tame	Proud	Submissive
Gentle	Mild	Calm
Peaceful	Selfish	Docile
Conceited	Confused	Humble

Notice that the above behaviors are ideally the outcome of an internal conviction. Furthermore, notice that in the preceding beatitudes, Jesus deals with the **deep** part of who we are. To fully understand what Jesus is teaching us, we must look at meekness in the setting in which Jesus is speaking, and also in the context of the previous beatitudes.

The meek will he guide in judgment: and the meek will he teach his way *(Psalms 25:9 KJV).*

"Blessed are the poor in spirit, for theirs is the kingdom of heaven. Blessed are those who mourn, for they will be comforted."

The working of the Holy Spirit in His sweet way causes me to have an internal revolution in my soul which results in the changing or *reorienting* of my priorities, goals, and values. My contact with the divine  redirects my internal ***compass*** so that my focus is off of myself as the primary concern and onto Him. He invites me to fellowship with Him. As I connect with Him, the God-designed hunger in my heart—that poverty of spirit—is satisfied.

After Jesus speaks about filling the hunger in our hearts, it is no coincidence that He introduces the concept of meekness. The meekness Jesus speaks of is initiated in our communion with God, and proceeds out of that fellowship. Then, it works its way to the external expressions identified earlier.

1. List some areas in your life where you are not particularly "meek."

_____

_____

_____

_____

_____

_____

2. A lack of meekness indicates areas in your heart in which you have a need or insufficiency. Ask God to show you what the core reasons are for these areas in your life. Write down what He is telling you.

_____

_____

_____

_____

_____

_____

_____

_____

•I want to encourage you to ask God to forgive you for the times and areas where you have not been meek—when your internal compass has been self-centered.

•Meekness is first in relation to God.

3. Write down all the memory verses you have learned so far in the following space:

_____

_____

_____

_____

_____

_____

_____

_____

_____

Practice today's memory verse at every red light you encounter as you drive around town.

_____

_____

Notes

Notes

Notes

Today's verse is Matthew 5:6: *"Blessed are those who hunger and thirst for righteousness, for they will be filled."*

Secrets

Lesson 8

The next three beatitudes, beginning with this lesson, address the outward evidence, or fruit, of the ongoing, personal relationship with God that the first three beatitudes portray.

Righteousness is defined as "one who is in right standing with God."

Tape a week's worth of verses on your bathroom mirror to review while brushing your teeth or "putting on your face."

"FOOD" FOR THOUGHT

- This beatitude is attached to the ones before it.

- Hungering and thirsting for righteousness means ardently looking for the character of God one is experiencing in one's heart.

- Hungering and thirsting for righteousness means having a desire to see the "right thing" done—the thing that would be pleasing to God.

- Righteousness is part of God's character.

Q&A

1. Why do you think Jesus said, "hunger and thirst" and not just "hunger" or "thirst"?

_____
_____
_____
_____
_____
_____
_____
_____

2. List some ways that one might "hunger and thirst for righteousness."

_____
_____
_____
_____
_____
_____
_____

3. Fill in the blanks with the proper word (I, me, my…) _____ am blessed when _____ hunger and thirst for righteousness, because _____ will be filled.

4. Reflect on the statement you just filled in and express your thoughts in the space below.

_____

_____

_____

_____

_____

_____

_____

_____

_____

_____

_____

_____

_____

Spend some time today reviewing Matthew 5:6.

BIBLE NOTE

God relates to us many times in Scripture by drawing parallels with food and eating. "Chew" on some of these "meaty" verses:

"How sweet are your words to my taste, sweeter than honey to my mouth!" (Psalms 119:103).

"When your words came, I ate them; they were my joy and my heart's delight, for I bear your name, O LORD God Almighty" (Jeremiah 15:16).

"Jesus answered, 'It is written: 'Man does not live on bread alone, but on every word that comes from the mouth of God' '" (Matthew 4:4).

" 'My food,' " said Jesus, " 'is to do the will of him who sent me and to finish his work' " (John 4:34).

"Like newborn babies, crave pure spiritual milk, so that by it you may grow up in your salvation, now that you have tasted that the Lord is good" (I Peter 2:2-3).

Notes

Notes

Notes

Today's verse is
Matthew 5:7:
*"Blessed are the
merciful, for they
will be shown
mercy."*

Secrets

Lesson 9

Since these beatitudes build upon the previous ones,
it is important to look at the previous verse and see
how it relates to the one we are investigating today.
In the former verse, we saw that God is a righteous
God—He wants the "right thing" done. If God were
only righteous with no mercy, we would all be dead.
Both characteristics—righteousness and mercy—
are reflective of who God is. God is balanced.

It is God's desire that we reflect His character. He
wants us to be both righteous (living a life of holiness
and uprightness) and merciful, all the while knowing
that without His grace and mercy, we would **never** be
capable of living in a way that pleases Him. God knows
the material with which He is working and He wants
us to reflect His character.

Q&A

1. In the space below, which characteristic—
righteousness or mercy—is easier for you to express
and why?

_____

_____

_____

_____

_____

_____

2. Why is the other characteristic not as easy to
express?

_____

_____

_____

_____

_____

_____

_____

A lot of times we struggle, trying to manifest something that we don't have. It's hard to give mercy, if we have never received mercy. It's hard to hunger and thirst for righteousness in this wicked society if we don't see an example (given in the Word) of a righteous God and begin to walk in righteousness.

"I rise before dawn and cry for help; I have put my hope in your word. My eyes stay open through the watches of the night, that I may meditate on *your promises"* (Psalms 119:147-148).

There is never a bad time to meditate upon the Word. Your day is filled with little moments here and there—standing in line at the grocery store, waiting for your children at their music lessons, commuting to work, commercials during the ball game— that you can use to meditate.

Time out!

3. Identify a time in your life when you received mercy and you didn't deserve it.

_____

_____

_____

_____

_____

_____

_____

_____

_____

_____

4. What impact did that have on you?

_____

_____

_____

_____

_____

_____

_____

_____

_____

5. List someone who needs mercy extended to them.

_____

_____

_____

_____

_____

6. Identify an area in your life where you need mercy.

_____

_____

_____

_____

_____

_____

_____

**Remember to review
ALL your verses.**

Notes

Notes

Notes

_____

_____

_____

_____

_____

_____

_____

_____

_____

_____

_____

_____

_____

_____

_____

_____

_____

_____

_____

_____

_____

_____

Today's verse is Matthew 5:8: *"Blessed are the pure in heart, for they will see God."*

Secrets

Lesson 10

This set of beatitudes in Matthew 5:7-9 speaks about hungering for righteousness, being merciful, and being pure in heart. They all deal with the fruit that is a direct result of our personal and continuous relationship with God.

One time I was struggling with insecurity, and was talking with God about my struggle. At one of my previous jobs, I was having a hard time feeling valuable, important, and significant. Hence, I was griping to God about my perceived lack.

God spoke to me through the first three beatitudes. He first took me to the beatitude that assures me of comfort. I complained to God that I was not feeling very *comforted* at that particular time. He dealt with me, agreeing that I was aware of my poverty of spirit:

> *"Blessed are the poor in spirit, for theirs is the kingdom of heaven"* (Matthew 5:3).

However, He also pointed out that I was mourning by lamenting my lack of significance:

> *"Blessed are those who mourn, for they will be comforted"* (Matthew 5:4).

In other words, I was looking for comfort from the wrong source. I was looking for *my work* to comfort me rather than the Holy Spirit—the Author of comfort. Consequently, I was having difficulty with

pride (the opposite of meekness) since I was attempting to gain encouragement and satisfaction through an insufficient source —my job. God showed me that if I would look to Him for comfort, I would be

When you first look at a new verse, write it out once completely. Then rewrite it, replacing some of the words with blank lines. Fill in the blanks later in the day.

Time out!

more settled, content, and fulfilled.

In verse eight, Jesus speaks of the *pure in heart.* The Greek word He used for *pure* is the same word from which we get our English word, *catharsis,* meaning "to make clean or to purge." The pure in heart reflect the character of Christ, Who is both righteous and pure. It is God's desire to see us live a righteous life, but He also knows that this is impossible without His grace and mercy. God wants us to be hungry to see righteous and moral results, but He also wants us to be merciful. After all, we are what we are (or are **not**) by His mercy.

Would you like to see God? Be pure in heart and mirror His character.

Q&A

1. List the second half of each of the beatitudes we have worked on so far:

_____

_____

_____

_____

_____

_____

_____

2. The list above expresses God's blessings to us. What, if any, of the list identified above do you *not* have?

_____

_____

_____

_____

_____

_____

_____
_____
_____
_____
_____

3. Why might you be lacking the blessing or blessings you identified?

_____
_____
_____
_____
_____
_____
_____

4. You are halfway through this study. At this point what verse has affected you the most? Why?

_____
_____
_____
_____
_____
_____
_____

_____
_____
_____
_____
_____
_____
_____
_____
_____
_____
_____

5. What have you learned about the kingdom of God that you did not know before you began meditating on the beatitudes?

_____
_____
_____
_____
_____
_____
_____
_____
_____

REVIEW

You are now at the end of Unit 2. Can you quote all eight of our memory verses? Write them out on the lines provided below.

_____

_____

_____

_____

_____

_____

_____

_____

_____

_____

_____

_____

_____

_____

_____

_____

_____

_____

_____

_____

_____

_____

Notes

Notes

Notes

9

Secrets

Unit Three

Your goal for
this week is
to memorize
Matthew 5:9-13.

"Blessed are the peacemakers, for they will be called sons of God. Blessed are those who are persecuted because of righteousness, for theirs is the kingdom of heaven. Blessed are you when people insult you, persecute you and falsely say all kinds of evil against you because of me. Rejoice and be glad, because great is your reward in heaven, for in the same way they persecuted the prophets who were before you. You are the salt of the earth. But if the salt loses its saltiness, how can it be made salty again? It is no longer good for anything, except to be thrown out and trampled by men" (Matthew 5:9-13).

Today's verse is
Matthew 5:9:
*"Blessed are the
peacemakers, for
they will be called
sons of God."*

Secrets

Lesson 11

Let's review the results we obtain from the beatitudes we have studied thus far. The first three beatitudes (Matthew 5:3-5) address the deep and ongoing relationship we can have with God.

The second set of beatitudes (Matthew 5:6-8) talks about how that deep and ongoing relationship affects our character, causing us to become merciful, pure in heart, and hungering and thirsting for righteousness. This second group also shows us the benefits of this relationship with God—becoming filled with righteousness, receiving mercy, and seeing God. Now we are going to see how putting these first two sets of beatitudes to work in our daily lives will affect our relationships with people.

As we begin to meditate on this last set of beatitudes dealing with our human relationships, we see that Jesus puts a premium on being a peacemaker—one who brings and/or makes peace.

Recently, I was in a meeting with some potentially explosive people, and I found myself becoming increasingly tense. During that time, I had also been trying to make it a priority to go through the Lord's Prayer on a daily basis in my devotions. One of the things I prayed and acknowledged in this devotion was that Jesus was my peace (Jehovah Shalom).

While I was sitting in this meeting feeling the tension escalating, I sensed Jesus quieting my heart. Instead of becoming part of the tension, Jesus was filling me with His peace, and I was able to stand above the stress. Jesus gave me peace, enabling me to be a *peacemaker*.

To be a peacemaker, you must know peace inside. Peace is an internal rather than an external reaction, and is accomplished through a relationship with the Author of Peace—Jesus.

Q&A

1. Take a minute here to ask Jesus to reveal some of His peace to you.

_____

_____

_____

2. Let's look at what it means to be a peacemaker through the following exercise. Picture yourself in a normally stressful situation you might encounter:

- perhaps you're running late for an important appointment, or...

- you have an ongoing conflict with a colleague at work or one of your neighbors, or...

- maybe there's a lot of tension between you and one of your children.

Picture your stressful situation and describe it in the following space:

_____

_____

_____

_____

_____

_____

_____

_____

3. Now, in the same stressful situation, how would a peaceful person behave? How would someone behave who is not internally shaken by the stress, conflict, or anxiety?

_____

_____

_____

_____

_____

_____

_____

_____

_____

Take another minute to reflect on the following scriptures and how they relate to you in your role as a *peacemaker*:

Isaiah 26:3: *"You will keep in perfect peace him whose mind is steadfast, because he trusts in you."*

Psalms 23:2-5: *"He makes me lie down in green pastures, he leads me beside quiet waters, he restores my soul. He guides me in paths of righteousness for his name's sake. Even though I walk through the valley of the shadow of death, I will fear no evil, for you are with me; your rod and your staff, they comfort me. You prepare a table before me in the presence of my enemies. You anoint my head with oil; my cup overflows."*

Micah 5:4,5: *"He will stand and shepherd his flock in the strength of the LORD, in the majesty of the name of the LORD his*

God. And they will live securely, for then his greatness will reach to the ends of the earth. And he will be their peace..."

John 14:27: *"Peace I leave with you; my peace I give you. I do not give to you as the world gives. Do not let your hearts be troubled and do not be afraid."*

Philippians 4:7: *"And the peace of God, which transcends all understanding, will guard your hearts and your minds in Christ Jesus."*

Use picture association.
Think of an outlandish picture to illustrate a scripture. The more outrageous, the better the image will stay in your mind. For example: *"Blessed are the poor in spirit, for theirs is the kingdom of heaven"* (Matthew 5:3). Imagine a very happy person in rags with empty pockets hanging inside out of his trousers. He is standing outside the gates of a glorious walled city that is opened to him. The mayor of the city is handing him the keys.

Say your verse aloud to yourself several times during the day.

Notes

Notes

Notes

Notes

Today's verse is
Matthew 5:10:
*"Blessed are those who
are persecuted because
of righteousness, for
theirs is the kingdom
of heaven."*

Secrets

Lesson 12

Notice how this beatitude has taken us from being a peacemaker into being persecuted. Isn't it interesting that Jesus puts both of these beatitudes immediately next to each other? I think it was His intention to convey an important message to us.

Do you remember from our study of verse six the meaning of *righteous*? Write it below.

_____

_____

_____

_____

_____

_____

Righteousness, in its simplest application, means to be in "right standing" with God—morally, ethically...and in all respects. Let's look at what this righteousness means in relation to the peacemaker and persecution beatitudes.

Sometimes a person will choose to be a peacemaker at the cost of his conscience. This kind of person folds under pressure—even when confronted with moral dilemmas. If he wanted to make peace at work, he wouldn't "rock the boat" when a moral crises arose. History shows us that before World War II, the British wanted peace with

Hitler. For the sake of peace, they were willing to stand aside and allow Hitler to invade Czechoslovakia, even knowing it was morally wrong. As a result, Hitler invaded not only Czechoslovakia, but also Poland, and started the Second World War.

Keeping the peace at all costs was not what Jesus had in mind, as is evidenced by this beatitude. Jesus did not want us to "give in" on issues related to righteousness. Doing the "right thing" is always a priority with Jesus, even if it means that we get some "heat" from those around us.

Q&A

1. In the following space, fill in your name or the appropriate second person pronoun (you, yours, etc.), then read back over your "revised" beatitude. Write your response to the revision in the space provided following your completed beatitude.

_____, _____ are blessed when

_____ are persecuted because of

righteousness, because _____ is the

kingdom of heaven.

_____

_____

_____

_____

_____

_____

_____

_____

_____

_____

_____

2. Let's examine how this beatitude relates to your life. Write down any instances that come to mind where you compromised in order to "keep the peace."

_____

_____

_____

_____

_____

_____

_____

_____

_____

_____

_____

_____

_____

3. Did that/those instance(s) compromise what you knew to be a moral issue? If so, what?

_____

_____

_____

_____

_____

_____

_____

_____

_____

_____

_____

_____

_____

_____

_____

If you have traded "peace" for something you knew to be morally wrong or unethical, I want to encourage you to take a few minutes here to ask God to forgive you and give you grace in future situations to make moral choices that remain consistent with righteousness, regardless of the persecution.

Here are some scriptures you may want to incorporate into your prayer time that will help strengthen you when faced with difficult moral dilemmas:

"The LORD is my strength and my shield; my heart trusts in him, and I am helped...." (Psalms 28:7).

"This is what the Sovereign LORD, the Holy One of Israel, says: 'In repentance and rest is your salvation, in quietness and trust is your strength,'..." (Isaiah 30:15).

"He gives strength to the weary and increases the power of the weak. Even youths grow tired and weary, and young men stumble and fall; but those who hope in the LORD will renew their strength. They will soar on wings like eagles; they will run and not grow weary, they will walk and not be faint" (Isaiah 40:29-31).

"The Sovereign LORD is my strength; he makes my feet like the feet of a deer, he enables me to go on the heights..." (Habakkuk 3:19).

"I can do everything through him who gives me strength" (Philippians 4:13).

"He will keep you strong to the end, so that you will be blameless on the day of our Lord Jesus Christ" (I Corinthians 1:8).

"And the God of all grace, who called you to his eternal glory in Christ, after you have suffered a little while, will himself restore you and make you strong, firm and steadfast" (I Peter 5:10).

Be sure to review all of your verses as you add new ones. At this point you should be reviewing Matthew 5:1-10 while you add verse 11.

Notes

Notes

Notes

_____

_____

_____

_____

_____

_____

_____

_____

_____

_____

_____

_____

_____

_____

_____

_____

_____

_____

_____

_____

_____

Today's verse is Matthew 5:11: *"Blessed are you when people insult you, persecute you and falsely say all kinds of evil against you because of me."*

Secrets

Lesson 13

Notice how this beatitude takes the issue of persecution a step further than the last beatitude. This is the first beatitude in which Jesus speaks directly to His audience, in a more conversational tone using "you, me." In the preceding beatitudes, Jesus spoke more generally—blessed are the meek, for they will inherit the earth. Let's look at the personal nature of this beatitude.

The words **when**, **you**, **me**, particularly impact me.

- Jesus says, **"when"** men persecute you—not if. When I'm walking closely with Jesus, it's not a case of *if* people will persecute me, but *when*.

- Jesus says, **"you."** This is the first place in the beatitudes where Jesus looks at me and says "you." When I repeat this verse, I see Jesus looking at me, and specifically saying that people will persecute you, Sarah (pointing to me).

• Jesus also says, **"me."** Jesus links Himself with me in a deeply personal way when I experience persecution.

While no one wants to be persecuted, I would prefer to experience persecution for a good cause rather than because of my foolishness. I am blessed when people connect me with Jesus and then harass me. I am not blessed when I experience trouble due to my own actions and behavior, but rather I am blessed when I receive opposition because of my association with Jesus.

Actually, Jesus says you are blessed when your connection to Him provokes people to insult, persecute, and speak evil about you.

Let's see what these words mean in the Greek:

- **insult:** *oneidizo*—to defame, i.e. rail at, chide, taunt: (In the KJV, it is translated as (suffer) reproach, revile, upbraid.)
- **persecute:** *dioko*—to chase you away or to oppose you
- **say all kinds of evil:** *poneros*—this means that evil, lewd, and malicious things are said about you. These rude things are said not about your character, but about the things you do.

Review your verses while you exercise. The Word says, *"For physical training is of some value, but godliness has value for all things, holding promise for both the present life and the life to come"* (I Timothy 4:8). As you walk, jog, lift weights, etc., practice the **MVPs** with your daily verse. That way, you'll be exercising your soul and spirit as you develop your physical body!

Q&A

In the following verse, circle the words that have an impact on you, and then explain how and why these words are affecting you:

"Blessed are you when people insult you, persecute

you and falsely say all kinds of evil against you

because of me."

_____

_____

_____

_____

_____

_____

_____

_____

_____

_____

_____
_____
_____
_____
_____
_____
_____
_____
_____
_____
_____
_____
_____
_____
_____
_____
_____
_____
_____

Can you quote *all* 11 verses now without looking? Try it out loud with a friend.

Notes

Notes

Notes

Today's verse is Matthew 5:12: *"Rejoice and be glad, because great is your reward in heaven, for in the same way they persecuted the prophets who were before you."*

Secrets

Lesson 14

When you are persecuted on account of Jesus, you are in good company. People have always come against Jesus and His message, as well as against the prophets in the Old Testament. If you are a part of the group that includes such godly saints, how could you not be blessed?

When you first look at a new verse, write it out once completely. Then rewrite it, replacing some of the words with blank lines. Fill in the blanks later in the day.

Q&A

Let's do some simple things to help learn this verse.

1. Read and say aloud verse 12.

2. Fill in the following spaces to the best of your ability without looking at the verse.

Rejoice and be _____, because great is

your _____ in heaven, for in the same

_____ they persecuted the _____

who were before _____.

3. Now read *out loud* the verse where you filled in the words.

4. Finally, in this last exercise, most of the words will be missing. To the best of your ability, fill in the blanks.

_____

and be _____,

_____ _____ is your _____

in heaven, _____ _____ _____ _____

_____ they _____

_____ _____ who were

_____ _____.

"By faith Moses...regarded disgrace for the sake of Christ as of greater value than the treasures of Egypt, because he was looking ahead to his reward" (Hebrews 11:24,26).

Take Inventory

Let's do an assessment of where we are so far in this study. In the beatitudes, we see that blessings come from certain behaviors and attitudes. For example, those who are pure in heart will see God (verse 8). In the box below, check the phrases that describe an area in your life where you seem to be lacking. Then, note the corresponding action or behavior that is linked to that blessing. The missing action or behavior could be largely responsible for the lack you have.

Consequence
__ having the kingdom of heaven
__ being comforted in life
__ inheriting the earth
__ having righteousness in life
__ acquiring mercy
__ seeing God
__ identified as a son of God
__ having the kingdom of heaven
__ great reward in heaven

I would also like you to see a progression in your inventory. Notice that the division of the beatitudes is in three groupings or focuses:
1. Our relationship with God
2. Our character as developed by the outworking of our relationship with God
3. Our relationships with others in the context of our connection with God.

I think if you'll view the inventory below in its progressive grouping that this will help you to focus on the particular areas that you may need to work on more.

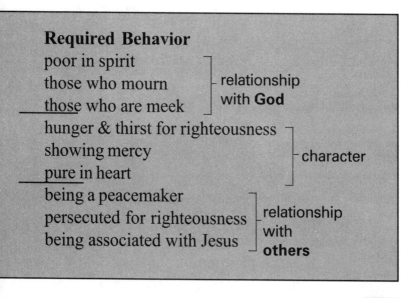

Required Behavior
poor in spirit
those who mourn ⎤ relationship
those who are meek ⎦ with **God**
hunger & thirst for righteousness ⎤
showing mercy ⎬ character
pure in heart ⎦
being a peacemaker ⎤ relationship
persecuted for righteousness ⎬ with
being associated with Jesus ⎦ **others**

Write out all the verses you have studied so far below.

_____
_____
_____
_____
_____
_____
_____
_____
_____
_____
_____
_____
_____
_____
_____
_____
_____
_____
_____
_____
_____

Notes

_____
_____
_____
_____
_____
_____
_____
_____
_____
_____
_____
_____
_____
_____
_____
_____
_____
_____
_____
_____
_____
_____
_____
_____
_____

Notes

Today's verse is
Matthew 5:13:
"You are the salt of the earth. But if the salt loses its saltiness, how can it be made salty again? It is no longer good for anything, except to be thrown out and trampled by men."

Secrets

Lesson 15

This verse is easy to visualize. To begin, picture yourself in a large salt shaker. Now imagine the salt shaker being turned upside down and you being shaken out—as if God were using you to "season" your environment. Now see yourself being used by God to bring **HIS** seasoning (saltiness) to the various places you go and to the different people you meet.

How do *you* taste to the people in your life?

_____

_____

_____

_____

_____

_____

_____

_____

_____

_____

_____

_____

_____

_____

Now, let's look at what the verse says about salt that is no longer salty. Imagine a salt shaker that appears to have salt in it. Picture yourself using this salt shaker to add some badly needed flavor to one of your favorite dishes. As you're putting the salt on the food, your mouth is watering because you

can't _wait_ to taste this delicious dish! You take your first bite and something seems to be missing, so you add some more salt, thinking that will help. You take your second bite, and the salt didn't seem to add

A good way to get these scriptures settled in your heart is to pray them back to the Father, either for yourself or a loved one. For example, you might pray, "Father, I thank You that when I am persecuted for Your sake, You have rewards and blessings set aside just for me. I thank You that I am not alone in this persecution; there is a long line of other godly men and women before me who have experienced this same persecution, too."

any flavor, so you look at the salt, pour a little in your hand to see if it's okay. You taste the "salt" in your hand and there's *no* flavor—no saltiness. That's discouraging! You get a little aggravated because the salt isn't salty. Who would mess with the salt and make it "un-salty"? That's a rude thing to do!

We, as Christians, are supposed to add flavor to our environment. If we do not add God's flavor, we are not really fulfilling God's purpose for our lives.

Q&A

1. How can people *"taste and see that the Lord is good,"* in your life if you have no flavor of Him—if you've lost your saltiness? Write your thoughts about this below.

_____

_____

_____

_____

_____

_____

_____

_____

_____

_____

_____

_____

_____

_____

_____

_____

How to be "salty":
- Stay around God a lot by reading the Word, talking to Him, worshipping Him.
- Don't back away from opportunities to be salty.
- Colossians 4:6, *"Let your conversation be always full of grace, seasoned with salt, so that you may know how to answer everyone."*
- Stay in church—keep your saltiness "stocked-up."
- Surrender to what God is doing in your life.

2. Think of some areas in your daily life that could use some seasoning and write down how you can be used by God to be "salt" in those situations or for those people.

_____

_____

_____

_____

_____

"Taste and see that the LORD is good; blessed is the man who takes refuge in him" (Psalms 34:8).

_____

_____

_____

_____

_____

_____

_____

_____

_____

3. Write what God is showing you about being "salty."

_____

_____

_____

_____

_____

_____

_____

_____

BIBLE NOTE
You Have a Destiny!

"This is what the LORD says— your Redeemer, who formed you in the womb: I am the LORD, who has made all things, who alone stretched out the heavens, who spread out the earth by myself,..." (Isaiah 44:24).

God created each of us with a specific call upon our lives. He told Jeremiah, *"...before you were born I set you apart; I appointed you as a prophet to the nations"* (Jeremiah 1:5).

Have you wondered what God *created* you to do while you are here visiting planet Earth? In the Sermon on the Mount, Jesus gives us each some answers. We are made salt and light. God designed us to be witnesses to the world of God's love and care for man. Don't let the devil tell you that you cannot be an effective witness—God fashioned you to succeed as salt and light even as He shaped Jeremiah to be a prophet.

Ask God to give you opportunities to fulfill the calls He has given you. Then look for ways to express His love to those around you.

REVIEW

We are at the three-quarter point in our workbook. The finish line is almost in sight!

What have you gained from meditating on the beatitudes? Do you have a bigger picture of God, a deeper understanding of who you are in Christ, or a greater appreciation for the Word? Spend a few minutes thinking about the benefits you have gotten from this study, and write them down or talk them over with a close friend.

_____

_____

_____

_____

_____

_____

_____

_____

Be prepared to recite Matthew 5:1-13, without looking at your Bible.

Notes

_____

_____

_____

_____

_____

_____

_____

_____

_____

_____

_____

_____

_____

_____

_____

_____

_____

_____

_____

_____

_____

_____

_____

_____

_____

_____

_____

Notes

_____

_____

_____

_____

_____

_____

_____

_____

_____

_____

_____

_____

_____

_____

_____

_____

_____

_____

_____

_____

_____

_____

Notes

Notes

9 Secrets

Your goal for
this week is
to memorize
Matthew 5:14-16.

"You are the light of the world. A city on the hill cannot be hidden. Neither do people light a lamp and put it under a bowl. Instead they put it on its stand, and it gives light to everyone in the house. In the same way, let your light shine before men, that they may see your good deeds and praise your Father in heaven" (Matthew 5:14-16).

Today's verse is
Matthew 5:14:
*"You are the light of
the world. A city on
a hill cannot be
hidden."*

Secrets

Lesson 16

In our fast-paced world, we often take light for granted. It is a very normal thing to walk into a dark room, casually flip the switch, and go about our business without giving the light a second thought. However, since God has called us to be light, may I challenge you to take light more seriously?

Jesus didn't just suggest that you could turn His light in you on and off. He said that, without reservation, *you are the light of the world.* In Jesus' day, light was provided by natural sources (sun, moon, stars) or from oil lamps. These lamps were filled with oil, had a wick, and provided light after sundown. These oil lamps were the ancestors of kerosene lamps.

The nice thing about this type of light was its simplicity. This light could burn forever if properly cared for with a continual supply of oil and wicks. Unlike modern light sources, the style of light that Jesus spoke about did not burn out like a light bulb, nor was it dependent upon some remote, unknown energy source.

As long as we keep our lives filled with the oil of the Holy Spirit and keep the flame of our relationship with our heavenly Father alive, we cannot be snuffed out!

Light Maintenance

A person in Jesus' time had a few simple, but important, tasks he needed to do to keep his oil light working well:

- Trim the wick—cut off the old, used wick. The unnecessary previously-burned wick would only defile the oil and impede the light.

- Keep fresh oil in the lamp—oil represents the anointing. If we do not stay fresh in God's anointing, we will use it up, run dry, and/or the oil will turn rancid. Check out Matthew 25:1-13.

- Keep the oil clean—don't let the oil become polluted or diluted. You can ruin or hinder the performance of the oil by adding things to it, thereby causing a variety of results including a smaller amount of light, strange fire (light), or a decreased amount of space in which the oil (anointing) resides.

If you have children with whom you share a daily or weekly devotional time, use a verse you are learning as the study scripture for the devotion. Plan a fun craft around it or use a memorable visual aid such as a salt shaker or a candle.

Let's work on personalizing this small, but profound, verse. In the following spaces, write the appropriate word (I, me, my) and, after completing the verse, go back and read what you have completed. As you read the amended verse, please take the time to ponder what you are reading, letting the meaning of the verse settle into you.

_____ (your name) _____

_____ the light of the world.
I am a city on a hill that cannot be hidden.

Notice also, that Jesus talks about *a* (single) light and then a whole *city of lights*. Let me challenge you to be involved with a church—a city on a hill that cannot be hidden. The church is a collection of single lights and, in its community, is intended to be **a city on a hill that cannot be hidden**.

Notes

_____

_____

_____

_____

_____

_____

_____

_____

_____

_____

_____

_____

_____

_____

_____

_____

_____

_____

_____

_____

_____

Don't forget! Review your new verse, Matthew 5:14.

Notes

Notes

Notes

Today's verse is
Matthew 5:15:
"Neither do people light
a lamp and put it under
a bowl. Instead they put
it on its stand, and it
gives light to everyone
in the house."

Secrets

Lesson 17

Here's an interesting verse about light. Jesus states the obvious—it is useless to turn on a light and then put it under a bowl! That's very silly and unthinkable. Perhaps the only time one would even consider hiding a light would be when doing something in secret. According to one Bible commentator, the only time a bowl was used to cover a light was when someone was doing something hidden or sinister. Jesus did not intend to put His light in us for us to be "renegade illumination." Instead, He fully intended for us to be a light in our communities to enable others around us to see the truth of Who Jesus is—the Savior of the world.

In the days of Jesus, there were small "shelves" that extended out a little bit from the walls of a home where oil lamps were placed so that the inhabitants would have light in their homes. In the same way, although the community around us may be in darkness, Jesus has placed us in our neighborhoods and environments to provide light. He has put us on our respective shelves, intending for us to be lights!

Let's look back over the verses we've covered so far and consider how they relate to each other. We see in the first three beatitudes that Jesus addresses the very core of who we are in relation to Him.

WE NEED GOD

Blessed are the poor in spirit, for theirs is the kingdom of heaven.

Blessed are those who mourn, for they will be comforted.

Blessed are the meek, for they will inherit the earth.

In the second grouping of the beatitudes, we see how our relationship with God affects us at the center of our souls and the way we evaluate things.

JESUS AFFECTS THE WAY WE PERCEIVE THINGS

Blessed are those who hunger and thirst for righteousness, for they will be filled.

Blessed are the merciful, for they will be shown mercy.

Blessed are the pure in heart, for they will see God.

Finally, in the third grouping of the beatitudes, we see that we not only need Jesus and that He affects the way we see things, but that our relationship with Him will also have an impact on our interpersonal relationships.

JESUS IMPACTS OUR RELATIONSHIPS

Blessed are the peacemakers, for they will be called sons of God.

Blessed are those who are persecuted because of righteousness, for theirs is the kingdom of heaven.

Blessed are you when people insult you, persecute you and falsely say all kinds of evil against you because of me.

Rejoice and be glad, because great is your reward in heaven, for in the same way they persecuted the prophets who were before you.

To boil all of this down, we see that there are three foundational principles expressed in the beatitudes. These are identified in the above groupings. Please list the three principles below:

1. _____

2. _____

3. _____

In verses 13-16, we read that we are salt and light. If we look at these verses in relation to the groupings of beatitudes immediately preceding these verses, it quickly becomes apparent that the salt and light descriptions are merely **extensions** of what Jesus said about our relationship with Him affecting our interpersonal relationships.

When Jesus discusses salt and light, He says that we are to have an impact on people we don't even know. Salt has a multitude of uses and is a very common element in life. In fact, salt is necessary for life. As for light, it is difficult to regulate where it goes and the impact it has—it just shines. Light is not selective—nor should we be selective with whom we share Jesus. Think about this: salt and light touch and affect everyone.

Fill in the following spaces:

I _____ salt.   _____ am light.

Here are some more powerful scriptures about light:

"You, O LORD, keep my lamp burning; my God turns my darkness into light" (Psalms 18:28).

"The light of the righteous shines brightly, but the lamp of the wicked is snuffed out" (Proverbs 13:9).

"For God, who said, 'Let light shine out of darkness,' made his light shine in our hearts to give us the light of the knowledge of the glory of God in the face of Christ" (II Corinthians 4:6).

Q&A

Think about three areas of darkness that you come in contact with during the week—a job situation, a school circumstance, etc. How can the light of Jesus change each one? Write your thoughts on the lines below and then pray about them, asking God to bring His light into the darkness.

_____

_____

_____

_____

_____

_____

_____

_____

_____

_____

_____

_____

_____

_____

REMEMBER
to review all of your verses
as you add new ones.

Notes

Notes

Notes

9 Secrets of Spiritually Successful People

Notes

Today's verse is
Matthew 5:16:
*"In the same way, let
your light shine
before men, that they
may see your good
deeds and praise
your Father in
heaven."*

Secrets

Lesson 18

In today's verse, Jesus continues teaching more about our calling to be lights to our generation. Just as the oil lamps were placed throughout the houses during Jesus' time to provide illumination, we are to shine before men with our good deeds **so that men may praise our Father in heaven.**

Unsaved people are earthly minded. They need to see, feel, or hear evidence that God exists and that He is good, loving, and kind. The apostle John understood this characteristic about men so well that he began his first epistle by relating his personal "hands-on" knowledge of Jesus:

That which was from the beginning, which

*we have **heard**, which we have **seen** with our eyes, which we have **looked** at and our hands have **touched**—this we proclaim concerning the Word of life. The life appeared; we have **seen** it and testify to it, and we proclaim to you the eternal life, which was with the Father and has appeared to us. We proclaim to you what we have **seen** and **heard**, so that you also may have fellowship with us....(I John 1:1-3)*

Have you ever heard the expression, "people need to see Jesus with flesh on"? When we walk in obedience to God, we will be doing His good works. Then, when the lost see our godly behavior, they will be drawn to Jesus in us.

How many times have we heard testimonies from people who came to Christ because they "saw" something different in a Christian? Very few people have a conversion experience as dramatic as the apostle Paul had (Acts 9); most of us were influenced by people God put in our paths who loved and served Him.

Record your memory verses on a cassette tape so you can play them throughout your day as you dress, do housework or yardwork, drive your car, etc.

Be prepared to go over all of your verses, including Matthew 5:16.

Reinforce your memorization by asking God to open His Word and to give you revelation knowledge.

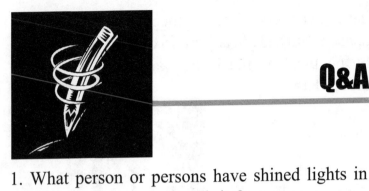

1. What person or persons have shined lights in your life that drew you to Christ?

_____

_____

_____

_____

_____

_____

_____

2. List below some things you could do that would cause others to look to God and give Him praise.

_____

_____

_____

_____

_____

_____

_____

_____

_____

_____

_____

_____

3. List below some things that you have seen other people do that have caused you to look at God and give Him praise.

_____

_____

_____

_____

_____

_____

_____

_____

_____

_____

_____

_____

_____

_____

_____

_____

4. Review your thoughts about the three dark areas from your life in the previous lesson. Has God shown you any way you can be salt and light in those dark situations? Write your thoughts down.

1._____

_____

_____

_____

2._____

_____

_____

_____

3._____

_____

_____

_____

Notes

Notes

Notes

Notes

Secrets

CONGRATULATIONS!
YOU DID IT!

You have finished the beatitudes—at least this time around. Don't throw this workbook away. Get it out and go through it again in a year or so. You'll be astounded at the new things the Holy Spirit will reveal to you. His Word is never ending in its scope and depth.

Q&A

1. Write out Matthew 5:1-16.

_____

_____

_____

_____

_____

_____

_____

_____

_____

_____

_____

_____

_____

_____

_____

_____

_____

_____

_____

_____

_____

_____

_____

_____

_____

_____

_____

_____

2. Ask someone close to you—a family member, friend, or memorization partner—what changes they have noticed in you since you started this workbook. Write them down on the lines below. They could be an encouragement to you in the future.

_____

_____

_____

_____

_____

_____

_____

_____

_____

_____

_____

ARE YOU READY FOR A NEW CHALLENGE?

Meditate (MVP) on these rich portions of scripture next. You will be blessed.

- **Moses' song of victory**
  —Exodus 15:1-18
- **A Psalm of exaltation**—Psalm 24
- **A Psalm of God's protection**
  —Psalms 40
- **Isaiah's portrait of Jesus our Substitute**—Isaiah 53
- **Jesus' prayer before the Crucifixion**—John 17
- **Our place in Christ**
  —Romans 6:1-14
- **Life through the Spirit**
  —Romans 8:1-11
- **Making our election sure**
  —II Peter 1:1-11

Brethren, I count not myself to have apprehended: but this one thing I do, forgetting those things which are behind, and reaching forth unto those things which are before, I press toward the mark for the prize of the high calling of God in Christ Jesus.

(Philippians 3:13-14)

Notes

Notes

_____
_____
_____
_____
_____
_____
_____
_____
_____
_____
_____
_____
_____
_____
_____
_____
_____
_____
_____
_____
_____
_____
_____
_____

Notes

Secrets

Lesson 20

Inventory Time

1. What has been particularly challenging to you through this study?

_____

_____

_____

_____

_____

_____

_____

_____

_____

_____

_____

_____

_____

_____

_____

_____

_____

_____

_____

_____

_____

_____

_____

2. What will you take with you permanently from
this study?

_____

_____

_____

_____

_____

_____

_____

_____

_____

_____

_____

_____

_____

_____

3. Have you recognized God transforming you in any particular way as you have soaked your soul in the beatitudes?

_____

_____

_____

_____

_____

_____

_____

_____

_____

_____

_____

_____

_____

_____

_____

_____

_____

_____

_____

_____

_____

_____

4. In what way do you feel you have become closer to God during this time?

_____

_____

_____

_____

_____

_____

_____

_____

_____

_____

5. List below the things God has spoken to you through this workbook.

_____

_____

_____

_____

_____

_____

_____

_____

_____

_____

_____

_____

_____

_____

_____

Notes

"Now when he saw the crowds, he went up on a mountainside and sat down. His disciples came to him,..." (Matthew 5:1).

"...and he began to teach them, saying:..." (Matthew 5:2).

"Blessed are the poor in spirit, for theirs is the kingdom of heaven" (Matthew 5:3).

"Blessed are those who mourn, for they will be comforted" (Matthew 5:4).

"Blessed are the meek, for they will inherit the earth" (Matthew 5:5).

"Blessed are those who hunger and thirst for righteousness, for they will be filled" (Matthew 5:6).

"Blessed are the merciful, for they will be shown mercy" (Matthew 5:7).

"Blessed are the pure in heart, for they will see God" (Matthew 5:8).

"You are the light of the world. A city on a hill cannot be hidden" (Matthew 5:14).

"Neither do people light a lamp and put it under a bowl. Instead they put it on its stand, and it gives light to everyone in the house" (Matthew 5:15).

"In the same way, let your light shine before men, that they may see your good deeds and praise your Father in heaven" (Matthew 5:16).

"Blessed are the peacemakers, for they will be called sons of God" (Matthew 5:9).

"Blessed are those who are persecuted because of righteousness, for theirs is the kingdom of heaven" (Matthew 5:10).

"Blessed are you when people insult you, persecute you and falsely say all kinds of evil against you because of me" (Matthew 5:11).

"Rejoice and be glad, because great is your reward in heaven, for in the same way they persecuted the prophets who were before you" (Matthew 5:12).

"You are the salt of the earth. But if the salt loses its saltiness, how can it be made salty again? It is no longer good for anything, except to be thrown out and trampled by men" (Matthew 5:13).

"Now when he saw the crowds, he went up on a mountainside and sat down. His disciples came to him,…" (Matthew 5:1).

"…and he began to teach them, saying:…" (Matthew 5:2).

"Blessed are the poor in spirit, for theirs is the kingdom of heaven" (Matthew 5:3).

"Blessed are those who mourn, for they will be comforted" (Matthew 5:4).

"Blessed are the meek, for they will inherit the earth" (Matthew 5:5).

"Blessed are those who hunger and thirst for righteousness, for they will be filled" (Matthew 5:6).

"Blessed are the merciful, for they will be shown mercy" (Matthew 5:7).

"Blessed are the pure in heart, for they will see God" (Matthew 5:8).

"You are the light of the world. A city on a hill cannot be hidden" (Matthew 5:14).

"Neither do people light a lamp and put it under a bowl. Instead they put it on its stand, and it gives light to everyone in the house" (Matthew 5:15).

"In the same way, let your light shine before men, that they may see your good deeds and praise your Father in heaven" (Matthew 5:16).

"Blessed are the peacemakers, for they will be called sons of God" (Matthew 5:9).

"Blessed are those who are persecuted because of righteousness, for theirs is the kingdom of heaven" (Matthew 5:10).

"Blessed are you when people insult you, persecute you and falsely say all kinds of evil against you because of me" (Matthew 5:11).

"Rejoice and be glad, because great is your reward in heaven, for in the same way they persecuted the prophets who were before you" (Matthew 5:12).

"You are the salt of the earth. But if the salt loses its saltiness, how can it be made salty again? It is no longer good for anything, except to be thrown out and trampled by men" (Matthew 5:13).

Receive Jesus Christ as Lord and Savior of Your Life.

The Bible says, *"That if thou shalt confess with thy mouth the Lord Jesus, and shalt believe in thine heart that God raised him from the dead, thou shalt be saved. For with the heart man believeth unto righteousness; and with the mouth confession is made unto salvation"* (Romans 10:9,10).

To receive Jesus Christ as Lord and Savior of your life, sincerely pray this prayer from your heart:

Dear Jesus,

I believe that You died for me and that You rose again on the third day. I confess to You that I am a sinner and that I need Your love and forgiveness. Come into my life, forgive my sins, and give me eternal life. I confess You now as my Lord. Thank You for my salvation!

Signed _____ Date _____

Mr. & Mrs.
Mr.   Please print.
Name Miss
Mrs. _____

Address _____

City _____ State _____ Zip _____

Phone (H)( ) _____

Write to us.
We will send you information to help you
with your new life in Christ.

Marilyn Hickey Ministries
P.O. Box 17340 • Denver, CO 80217 • 303-770-0400
www.mhmin.org

Prayer Request(s)

Let us join our faith with yours for your prayer needs. Fill out the coupon below and send to Marilyn Hickey Ministries, P.O. Box 17340, Denver, CO 80217.

Prayer Request(s) _____

_____

_____

_____

_____

_____

Please print.

Name Mr. & Mrs.
      Mr.
      Miss
      Mrs. _____

Address _____

City _____

State _____Zip _____

Phone(H) (   ) _____

     (W) (   ) _____

If you want prayer immediately, call our Prayer Center
at 303-796-1333, Monday–Friday,
4 a.m.–4:30 p.m. (MT).

Marilyn Hickey Ministries

Marilyn was a public school teacher when she met Wallace Hickey. After their marriage, Wally was called to the ministry and Marilyn began teaching home Bible studies.

Marilyn and Wally adopted their son Michael. Then through a fulfilled prophecy they had their daughter Sarah who, with her husband Reece Bowling, is now part of the ministry.

The vision of Marilyn Hickey Ministries is to "cover the earth with the Word"(Isaiah 11:9). For more than 30 years, Marilyn Hickey has dedicated herself to an anointed, unique, and distinguished ministry of reaching out to people—from all walks of life—who are hungry for God's Word and all that He has for them. Millions have witnessed and acclaimed the positive, personal impact she brings through fresh revelation knowledge that God has given her through His Word. Marilyn has been the invited guest of government leaders and heads of state from many nations of the world. She is considered by many to be one of today's greatest ambassadors of God's Good News to this dark and hurting generation. The more Marilyn follows God's will for her life, the more God uses her to bring refreshing, renewal, and revival to the Body of Christ throughout the world. As His obedient servant, Marilyn desires to follow Him all the days of her life.

Marilyn founded her ministry "Life for Laymen" so that she could reach more people with her gift for practical Bible application.

Marilyn taught at Denver's "Happy Church"—now Orchard Road Christian Center (ORCC)—and hosted ministry conferences with husband Wally, pastor of ORCC.

At a retreat in 1976, Marilyn realized she was called to "cover the earth with the Word."

The ministry staff in the early days helped Marilyn answer the mail that came in response to her first 15-minute radio show.

Soon Marilyn realized she could reach more people through television. She and Wally hosted many well-known guests.

In Guatemala with former President Ephraim Rios-Mott

Marilyn has been the invited guest of government leaders and heads of state from many nations of the world.

In Egypt with Mrs. Anwar Sadat

In Venezuela with former first lady Mrs. Perez

Marilyn ministered to guerillas in Honduras and brought food and clothing to the wives and children who were encamped with their husbands.

The popular Bible reading plan *Time With Him* began in 1978 and invited people to "read through the Bible with Marilyn." The monthly ministry magazine has since been renamed *Outpouring*. It now includes a calendar of ministry events, timely articles, and featured product offers.

Through Word to the World College (formerly Marilyn Hickey Bible College), Marilyn is helping to equip men and women to take the gospel around the world.

Sarah Bowling taught at Riverview Christian Academy for several years before her marriage, wrote correspondence courses for the Bible college...and has since joined the ministry full-time where she combines teaching at WWC with ministry trips and crusades.

God opened doors for the supplying of Bibles to many foreign lands—China, Israel, Poland, Ethiopia, Russia, Romania, and the Ukraine, just to name a few.

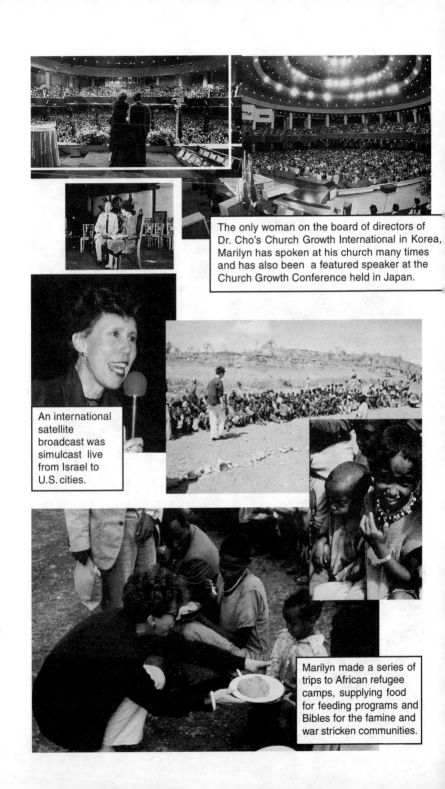

The only woman on the board of directors of Dr. Cho's Church Growth International in Korea, Marilyn has spoken at his church many times and has also been a featured speaker at the Church Growth Conference held in Japan.

An international satellite broadcast was simulcast live from Israel to U.S. cities.

Marilyn made a series of trips to African refugee camps, supplying food for feeding programs and Bibles for the famine and war stricken communities.

Sarah began traveling overseas with her parents at an early age and developed a heart for missions.

Both Marilyn and Sarah have a strong heart for China, and have distributed thousands of Bibles and tracts there and in Russia.

The ministry expanded from its beginnings in a cardboard box of files on a kitchen table, to the first International Ministry Center, built in 1985, to its present headquarters located in Greenwood Village, Colorado.

FILL THE SHIP, a special project of the Marilyn Hickey Children's Fund, supplies food and Bibles to various Third World countries, such as Haiti, the Philippines, Ethiopia, Honduras, and El Salvador.

The prime time television special, "A Cry for Miracles," featured co-host Gavin MacLeod.

Marilyn has been a guest several times on the 700 Club with host Pat Robertson.

Marilyn ministered in underground churches in Romania before any of the European communist countries were officially open.

Marilyn Hickey's Prayer Center handles calls from all over the U.S.— ministering to those who need agreement in prayer.

More than 1,500 ministry products help people in all areas of their life.

Marilyn received her honorary doctorate from Oral Roberts University. She now serves as the chairman of the Board of Regents.

Sarah graduated from ORU, and later earned her Masters in History.

Marilyn and her Faith Covenant Partners respond to countless needs across the world. . .the devastating earthquakes in Mexico City, Romanian orphans, leprosy victims in Africa, orphans in war torn Rwanda, street children in Brazil,. . . all are touched by God's power.

MHM supports Mission of Mercy in Calcutta, headed by Huldah Buntain. Marilyn has made several trips there.

Airlift Manila provided much needed food, Bibles, and personal supplies to the Philippines; MHM also raised funds to aid in the digging of water wells for those without clean drinking water.

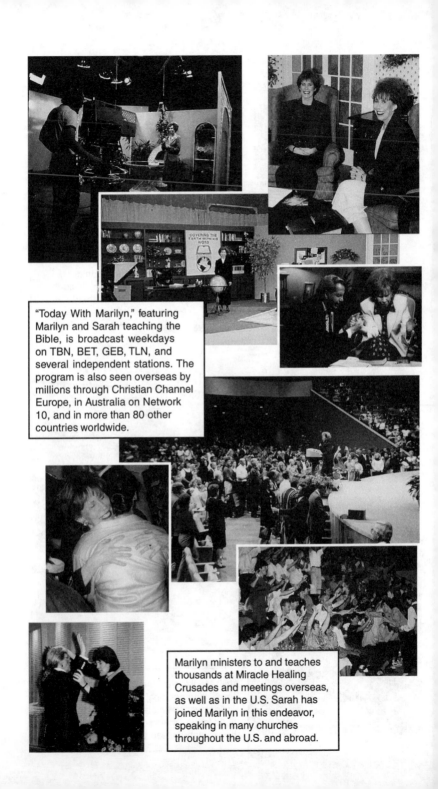

"Today With Marilyn," featuring Marilyn and Sarah teaching the Bible, is broadcast weekdays on TBN, BET, GEB, TLN, and several independent stations. The program is also seen overseas by millions through Christian Channel Europe, in Australia on Network 10, and in more than 80 other countries worldwide.

Marilyn ministers to and teaches thousands at Miracle Healing Crusades and meetings overseas, as well as in the U.S. Sarah has joined Marilyn in this endeavor, speaking in many churches throughout the U.S. and abroad.

Exciting ministry opportunities awaited Marilyn, Sarah, and their team of travelers in the Ukraine and Russia, as the doors opened for the Gospel.

Victim of the nuclear power plant disaster in Chernobyl

Marilyn has held Bible Encounters in Malaysia and Singapore. While traveling through Hong Kong she ministered to Vietnamese in a refugee camp.

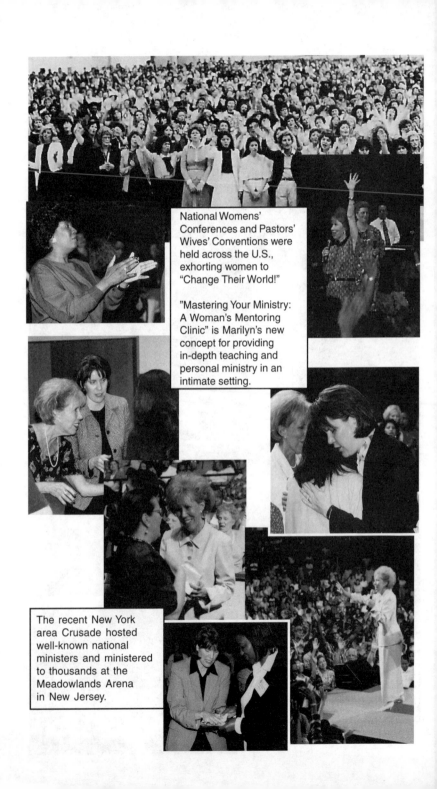

National Womens' Conferences and Pastors' Wives' Conventions were held across the U.S., exhorting women to "Change Their World!"

"Mastering Your Ministry: A Woman's Mentoring Clinic" is Marilyn's new concept for providing in-depth teaching and personal ministry in an intimate setting.

The recent New York area Crusade hosted well-known national ministers and ministered to thousands at the Meadowlands Arena in New Jersey.

Ministry trips and cruises to places such as Indonesia, China, Russia, Greece, the Ukraine, Turkey, Africa, and Israel offer short-term missions' opportunities to travel to exotic places and minister with Marilyn and Sarah.

MHM overseas offices now operate in the United Kingdom, Australia, and South Africa. Marilyn and Sarah also host yearly meetings, Crusades, and missions' projects in those countries.

Crowds of up to 200,000 attended the open-air Crusade in Bangalore, India.

In Islamabad, Pakistan, Marilyn held Ministry Training Schools. Total Crusade attendance was estimated at 70,000.

Ministry Training Schools are held in many Third World countries, such as Sudan and Tanzania, and provide training and native language literature for local pastors and church leaders. Nightly Crusades are held to minister to the local populations.